Keep on treading…

... the sun's about to rise.

Cuerpo Y Alma Publishing
New York

An Enlightened Lunatic In Verse And Prose

Originally Published On March 30th, 2015
ISBN: 069241875X
ISBN-13: 978-0692418758 (Cuerpo y Alma Publishing)
Printed in the United States of America

AN ENLIGHTENED LUNATIC IN VERSE AND PROSE

Gabriel Weiner

Also by Gabriel Weiner

The Gift: Appreciate Who You Are Again

May each verse and each prose
Bring you closer to yourself

Thank You

ᛞ

God, Mami, Daddy, Fabie, Benji, Aarón, Andrés, Mamá, Grandma, Papá, Grandpa, Alba, Sam, Martie, Allan, Amy, Beth, Sasha, Bobby, Chan, Reyna, El Jeep, Spankie, Spotty, Cookie, White Socks, Mecho, Clara, Chelo, Momín, María Del Carmen, Pili, Isa, Kathy, Gundo, Kiki, Charo, Tiguí, Juan, Chichí, Raque, Lía, Hendry, María, Eric, Jairo, Argenis, Wascar, Tella, Fifa, Tana, Chila, La Morena, Quisqueya, Papo, Carmela, Arelis, Ana, Javier, Dionys, Augusto, Julián, Carmen, Caraballo, Pinea, José Julio, Jimmy, Edgar, Nieves, Ismael, Miguelito, Jorleny, El Profe, Junior, Rafael, Luis, Cuca, Karina, Julio, Idelza, José, Kenia, Giselle, Dayhana, Sr. Curiel, El Moro, Amanda, Edniza, Leo K, Ricky, Robi, Diego, El Calvo, Rafie, Michelle, Ambar, Susana, Samuel, Leonardo, Titi, Chin, Félix, Paola, Moisés, Linneth, Jonás, Ms. Randolph, Fritz, Oliver, Doña Nena, Dona, Steve, Lindsay, Johnny, Marino, Gladys, Alejandro, Sonia, La Tote, Teresa, Freddy, Karen, Carrie, Phil F, Prof. Lipton, Milton, Kathy, Ryan, Laura, Mark B, Samara, Kyle, Rachael, David, Tiffany, Rachel, Stephen, LaNette, Nieves, Ro, Jenna, Holly S, Tim, Liz, Lauren, Adam L, Otis, Chris C, Dale, Deepak, James P, Danny, Marc, Mark, David, Seth, Breck, David J, Michael M, Jeannie, John, Brian, Dante, Irine, Phil, Ralph Waldo, Noah, Adam K, Eckhart, Adyashanti, Nisargadatta, Larry, Scott, Mike, Mokshananda, Aiden, Julia, Kim M, Jesús, Siddhartha, Sue, Tom, Henry, Gunther, Joey, Jean Carlos, Jeremy, Jackson, Yajaira, Yanybel, Luis Angel, Manito, Byron K, Jeffrey, Anabel, Oscar, Pedro, Elizabeth, Joey, Grant, Mia, Betsy, Cruise, Josh, David H, Ramana, Gangaji, UG, Kean, Cathy, Cecilia, Ben, Carlos, Vicky, Jenny, Marcelo, Rossanna, Leilany, Natalie, John S, Euny, Edilene, Mita, Pat, Benjamin S, Charlie, Matt, Jon, Craig, Florian, Catherine, Loch, Rick, Leonard, Stephan, Oswaldo, Holly, Boaz, Mor, Benny, Max, Jeff, Mike Q, Inelia, Timothy, Carole, Sara, Ash, Sandro, Ashley, Allan, Esther, Américo, Bella, Akhil, Bri, Matt, Michael, Natali, Sydney, Jeffrey, Troy, Israel, Dariusz, Rupaul, Víctor, Mia C, Sabrina, Kaitlyn, Stephanie, Allayah, Olivia, Corinne, Cass, Heather, Ana, Arianna, Ryan, Nina, Agnieszka, Wioleta, Dorota, Richard C, Robert, Mukti, Cheri, Dave, Bob, Carole S, Jen, Justin, Chris, Jen Y, James P, Ana J, Daniel S, Leonardo G, Megan, Yohanna, Ole, Domingo, Greilyn, Paul A...

Table of Contents

𝒫

III. Third Quarter: Alchemy

IV. Full Moon: Integration

V. Dawning: Nirvana

Prayer

May I never forget that I was once young and dumb.
May I never again be desperate for applause or praise.
May I never again compete or compare.
May I never again close my ears or my heart.
May I never again judge anyone (including myself.)
May I never value anything over the present moment.
May I never again avoid reality, even when it hurts.
May fear or hatred never be in charge of my life.
May I never again struggle to be perfect.
May I never again impose harsh demands on others.
May I never again play the victim.
May compassion always be number one in my life.
May I never use my own wisdom against myself.
May I never again lack patience, faith or willingness.

Amen.

Introduction

Hi, I'm Gabriel and I want to share some of my poetry with you. But before I do that, I want to give you a little bit of background about where the poetry in this particular book comes from. You see, I've always been a pretty sensitive guy, very curious and a lover of thinking and feeling... you know, harmless things, right? Well yes, but that's only until you run into people with ideas and beliefs that tell you the opposite. People who believe that being a man and being sensitive just don't go together, that curiosity is not good (after all, it killed the cat, didn't it?) and that thinking "too much" is bad for you.

Should I turn my curiosity off? Should I stop thinking? Should I stop being sensitive? These were some of the deep questions that kept running inside of me for a good chunk of my teen and tween years. It was torturous. My head just kept spinning around in circles. And so for many years, I was trying to figure out the answers to these questions in a pretty desperate (yet mostly quiet) way.

Luckily for me, the answers started to become available in the summer of 2007 when I had an experience that made the expression of most of the poems in this book possible. It was a profound and intense spiritual awakening that forced my heart and psyche to open up so that I could finally express the buildup of thoughts and emotions stuck within my gut. Finally! A crack in the iceberg of frozen and unexamined feelings, doubts, questions, beliefs and ideas that kept silently torturing me in ways I wasn't even aware of.

Thanks to this blessed awakening I started to be able to truly see what was buried within and so, I was finally able to put those dug up monsters and blessings into words. I cherish this awakening a lot, and that's because I deem it to have been the beginning of the end of the incessant circular battle that was occurring within me. Little by little I was able to open up to the emotional fire, wind, water, earth and spirit that partially constitute the person that I am.

As I see it now, the most important fact and gift of all is that this powerful awakening marked the beginning of the end of my ability to value anything that isn't truly important or real to me. And so this very blessed and cherished awakening has greatly started and continues to heal and nourish my heart and soul through time.

I thank you deeply for your interest and attention and I hope you enjoy.

Blessings,

Gabriel Weiner
Westwood, NJ
March 2015

New Moon:
Purification

Out

Around such pathetic idiots
They make me feel so red
They are so frozen
Like dolls
There's no zest
No life in their artificial world
It's so nineteen fifties
I hate it
I'm expelling myself out of this muck
It's repulsive to me
I'm no longer inclined
I'm out

Crazymakers

Unable to practice
So able to preach
They dress their ignorance
In a suit of shaky wisdom

They dress their pain
In a suit of artificial strength
They love to shout

They are the ones who take Tylenol
Yet say they never do

They have it together for all but themselves

Their age and their stuff
Inflate their empty heads
And when they have a job and a plan
They're even worse

Their food of choice is another's weakness
And they call this love

Have some dignity
It's not too late
Turn your eyes around
Stop it

Be exactly who you want me to be
And show me how to do it

Clown Club

There's a card
You might have
And not know it
If you stand in to defend cowards
You're a member
You're afraid
It's not okay to be a prick
And it's not okay to be a dick
I say so
And if you don't like my message
Go fuck yourself
For you're a dick
A prick
An asshole
I'm not a member of your club
And if I have to break you and break myself for it
I'll do it
Quit your shit
You petty idiot
Grow the fuck up
You're destroying the planet

Let Me Guess

You think you're the only one
You're a self-centered idiot
You're so fucking predictable
You make me sick to my stomach
I'm so bored of your crap
You don't do unconditional love
The universe revolves around you
You make me so sick
You have no clue
You're poisoning the planet
Turning it all into your petty bullshit
I'm so sick and tired of you
I'm breaking out of your bullshit
I find you repulsive
If you're reading this
I'm talking to YOU
Not anyone else
Cry and bitch
Feel the holy water splash
For you're a demon
A monster
Disappear out of existence
You destructive piece of crap

The Ultimate Insult

Label me not
For it's an insult of the highest order
Not only to me
But also to you
For I am not what you believe me to be
And what you believe me to be is too small to be
true

I am not a poet
I am not an artist
I am not a son
I am not a brother
I am beyond all
I am not arrogant
I am not an egomaniac

I, my beloved, simply am
And so are you

So insult yourself not
And quit putting yourself in boxes
For boxes are for things
And you are not a thing
You are not good
You are not bad
You simply are

Beyond words, beyond symbols
Beyond the idea of beyond

Quit the game of killing
For that is what you do when you pretend to know
For all you know is you know nothing
And you don't even know that

The chances of this making sense to a frozen mind
Are zero
But if you sense beyond what you know
You will be still
And come to know

Absolutely NOT

I refuse to play your games
I say hell no to hell
I'm not interested in swimming in your polluted
waters
Drama is boring as can be

I will not dance with you anymore
I will not listen to your nonsense
I will not play any fucking more

NO! Absolutely NOT!
I am not part of the machine
I am not destroying along with you
I am not interested in the least

NO more
Fuck off
Go away
Break off

You are boring as can be
You are an endless pit
You are a monster

All you do is argue
All you do is fight
All you do is conflict
All you do is pain
All you do is hurt

NO MORE
ABSOLUTELY NOT!

You know fear
I know love
You know illusion
I know reality

You know drama
I know simple

You know mind
I know Mind

Absolutely, positively NO!
NO! NO! NO!
I am NOT playing anymore
I don't CARE!

I am out!
I am done!
I don't want you anymore!
Fuck off!
Absolutely NOT!
I won't play your games!
NOT EVER AGAIN!
NEVER!

Society

Save your thoughts
For I no longer need them
Your compliments
You criticisms
They mean lick to me

I stand alone
I am free
I am all I need
You should try it
It's so very sweet

You are no longer my mirror
You are no longer my star
You are no longer my sun
You are just a smoked cigar

Think what you want
Bitch as you'd please
Say what you think
Scream all you need

Goodbye
Until never
I know who I am
Good luck to you

Swing

Up, down, up, down
Left, right, left, right
Good, bad, good, bad

The swing of this pendulum
Is making me dizzy
It feels like a wacky video game
I need to abandon my wishes
Of holding on to either part of the swing

This is crazymaking
It's so exhausting
It's annoying as can be

Yet the swings keep happening
It's so bipolar
I need a reminder that all is well
No matter where the pendulum is

I'm tired
Exhausted
Cansado

There is nothing I can do!

Issues

Sentimental or not
I no longer see
Value in your issues
Mine are even closer and I see them as unreal

Stories no longer buy me
Since thanks to grace
I'm here and mostly here

I don't listen
And you don't even notice
Because you don't even notice me

And it's okay
Because I don't notice you either
I'll go further
You don't even notice yourself

It all must be because
You are there
And I am here
Absolutely here

Annoyed Philosopher

I'm not afraid of death
For I don't fear things that don't exist
It's the things that appear to exist
That have the power to delude me into fear

What's all this massive immaturity about?
Is there an answer?
Nothing I can know, I'm sure
Why is my father playing cards on his computer all
day?
Why does it affect me and bother me SO much?

What is this reluctance to pain all about?
It's so childish, so absurd, so ridiculous
Why is the world in a teenaged mindset?
Why do I care so DEEPLY about these things?
Why does it affect me so much?
Why doesn't it affect YOU as much as it affects me?

Why can I walk into my feelings and assume
responsibility for them?
Why can't you?
What the fuck are you so god damn afraid of?
What is your PROBLEM?
When will you grow up?
Why do I care SO MUCH?
Why don't you?

What is it you want that is not maturity, wisdom

and purity?
What could possibly be more appealing to you?

Sweet Imminent Death

Push, I will
As much as need be
Drive as hard
Crash as fast
Break
Collapse
Dissolve

I will push myself
Until I'm totally done
It's what I am
And if I must shout I will
At the price of my throat
I will wake up
And die

In Process

They call themselves in check
Because they're boring
They always talk about the same thing

They call themselves sane
Because they suppress their reflexes
And when they blow up
It's because we're crazy

Is loving to create crazy?
It's true
Creation is organized chaos
And to organize chaos, we have to abandon the
traditional

So who's crazy?
The one that becomes numb to real stimuli?
Or the one who responds to the subtleties of
reality?

Who's crazy?
The one who suffers for real injustice?
Or the one that blinds himself to survive?

What's crazier?
Being able to see
Or blinding oneself?

We may all be crazy

The blind and the seers
But I'd rather see and be crazy
Than be blind and call myself sane

Awaken or Bust

The irrational drive towards enlightenment
Gives you no choice
It answers the choice/no choice dilemma
With this true, authentic impulse
You find out that you have NO CHOICE
But to awaken
To realize yourself fully
It will not let up
Until it happens
Ever
When it's time, it's time

It is not a choice for those who are ready
For those who are caught

Awaken or bust

The Soup In Which We Struggle

I feel so bored
I am so tired
I am so alone
Life is unfair
I hate living
Life sucks
I'm so confused
I don't know what I want
I don't know who I am
I'm depressed
I feel like shit
I want to die
I'll never amount to anything
I'm no good
No one loves me
I am a loser
I suck
I want today to be over
I don't like this
I don't want this
This isn't it
I feel terrible
I don't feel good
I don't get it
I have no friends
I have no life
I'm a total failure
I'm the biggest loser
I want to die

Manic Enlightenment Bug

There's a bug inside of me
Ravaging all of me
It's destroying me
And there's nothing I can do about it
I can't even fucking really write anymore
Get this over with
I'm fucking exhausted, tired and fed up
Enough self-seeking
I'm fucking done
Please leave me alone
Please
I can't anymore
Or can I keep going?

Only those with this impulse driving them
Have a clue of what I'm talking about

The Me's Kick and Scream Song

I'm not giving up
Ever
I'm real
I will continue and fight and struggle and strain
and push
Forever
I will make it to the end
I will break through
I will understand
I will reach heaven
I will be at peace
I am so real
I am all that is real
I am in charge
I know how to do this
Without me, there would be nothing
I am the center of the universe
I am all there is
I know
I will win
I will go on
I will forge through
I will break

Drive

I will shout until I can't shout no more
I will write until I'm emptied out completely
I will cry until there's no more tears
I will laugh until I'm out of life
I will dance until I have no feet
I will sing until the voice falls out
I will not cave in
I will not surrender
I will win the impossible battle
I will break the gates of heaven
And enter like a maniac
Like a psycho
Like a schizo
Like a nut
I will be laughed at, mocked
And I will forge on through
No one and nothing can stop me
Ever
Never, ever
I will keep this insanity going
Until the lights are out

Insecure Rock Star

I want to make you jealous and prove to you that
I got it and you don't
I want you to want to be like me but not be able to
because it is impossible
I want you to fight for what I fought for and seek
what I sought
I don't want you to find it
For if you do
Then you won't be of any use to me

I want you to admire me, respect me and love me
I want you to put me up high on a pedestal
I want to be your hero, your king, your God, your
guru, your teacher

I want to be on top and I want you to be at the
bottom
This is why I write all this nonsense that I'm
always writing
This is why I'm always blabbering about all the shit
I know

I want you to think I'm cool and want to be like me
I need fans, I need to be needed
This is why I share this stuff with you

It's all about me

Untitled

Go on and tell me how everything I have I owe to
you
And how I was put on this earth to make you
proud
Go on and break my heart and step on it yet once
again
Tell me what to do, tell me what to be
Tell me what to say, tell me when to breathe

Kill me
Step on me
Make me yours
Be a man and tell me what you mean
Tell me how much you hate me for not being like
you

Dump it all on me
Blame me, spit on me, step on me
And you too
Tell me how I owe life to you
Put all the blame, all the guilt and all the shame in
and on me
Tell me how useless and selfish I am
Give me all the blame
Remind me that I'm a demon, a devil, a piece of
shit
Tell me how I get it all from your mothers

You two are too wise

Everything you touch gets turned to gold
I should aspire to be just like you two
Two living luminaries

Ode to Hate

There is nothing I can do to keep enlightenment
from dawning
It's way too late
I was destined to be self-realized
From the day that I was born

There is nothing I could do to see the world
through a distorted filter
There is nothing I can do to run away from myself
anymore
This is absolutely inevitable
The crash will happen
And it will all be done
It will be like a dream that ended
It will be drama free
It will be ordinary
It will be sublime
It will mean nothing

This is so stupid
I hate having insane parents
I hate having insane brothers
I hate having an insane sister
I hate being insane and knowing I'm insane
I hate hating and knowing that it's all self-hatred

I hate being smart
I hate being handsome
I hate being awake

I hate life
I hate the world
I hate existence
I hate everything

This is so stupid and pointless
I'm surrounded by so many idiots
I'm surrounded by so many jerks
I hate being so damn clear

I hate what I see and live and I don't want to accept
it
The world sucks
I hate life
I hate this place
I hate this

Untitled

Hit me so hard that I can't take it
Shoot me
Kill me
I'm ready
I swear

I want you to hit me, hit me hard
Bite me, have no mercy
Destroy me
Eat me

I am ready
Come on in
And destroy me

A Naked Me's Confession

I want to be famous
I want to be asleep and I want to be awake
I want it all
I want to get away with all the shit I do

I want the dream and I want the Truth
I want to get in great shape
I want to feel good
I don't want pain and suffering

I just want pleasure
I just want good times and good moments
I don't want the bad stuff
I want to keep judging, blaming, accusing, pointing
fingers and avoid taking full responsibility
I want the dream more than I want the Truth

I want to make excuses
I want to have reasons to whine and complain
I want to keep believing that I am real
But I am not

I want to stay in charge, I want control, I want
power
I don't want the Truth, yet I do
But I don't want to give up
I don't want to give myself up

I want to own life

I want to get away with all my nonsense
I don't want to fully wake up
This is how I feel, this is what I want

I don't want to be That
I want to be whatever bullshit I make up
I'm kidding myself pretending to be honest and
earnest
I am not

I am a
Screw this

Ego Nausea

The puke wants to burst out
When I think of how
There's an idiotic no
To what's so

I have no idea where these poems come from
I am pretty disconnected
But the nausea brings me home
By taking me out of ego

Thank God for nausea
Thank God for puke
Thank God for discomfort
Thank God for suffering
Thank God for wow

It's amazing how the body
Just knows
If it's here or if it's not
When it's here, it is here
And not there

Heavy Energy

Game spoiler
Life distortioner
Truth clouder
Joy, clarity and creativity zapper

Lie promoter
Mind annoyer
Heart closer
Fear lover

Death seeker
Pain believer
Harm conceiver
Cynic, questioner, doubter, seeker, looker
Obsessive-compulsive dread story maker

Heavy energy
Life sucker
Lazy provoker
Depression, illness and fight lover

Forgetter of truth
Forgetter of the game
Forgetter of the joke
Massive ego fuel
Heavy, heavy, heavy, serious, serious, heavy stuff

Pessimistic
Nihilistic

Believer in doom and gloom
Heavy, heavy energy
See it, drop it, leave it

Lighten Up

It's all a fucking act
Get over it people
It's not real
It's not serious
It's not going anywhere
It's not important

It's just a fucking act
A game
A play
A show
None of it is real
It's just appearance

It's irrelevant
It's not serious
It's more like a joke
Enjoy it
Laugh

First Quarter:
Detachment

My Little World

My little world
Has been delicious
I've gotten away with more than I thought I could
I fooled everyone
Including myself
I danced on a ball
And it felt very safe

My little world
Is collapsing into the truth
My little world
Is fading

My little world was so sweet
But now it's time to be
And say goodbye
To my little world

Untitled

Nothing sticks anymore
It's all sucked into nothingness

I can't even write this poem
It's all gone

Groundless

The ground beneath my feet has been seen through
There is nothing here
Just infinite and eternal space

I am totally awake
And it's no big deal
It's so ordinary
It means absolutely nothing

Identity

It's not that you lose your identity
It's that you realize that there is no identity
You realize that absolutely nothing is true outside I
AM

The content is the dream
The play, the stuff

Truth, Peace, Joy, Love, Wisdom, Beauty are
inherent in what I am
They are not anywhere but eternally here now

There is no identity
There is no self
There is nothing but I AM

Glimpse

Heaven keeps tasting itself
It's got nothing to do with me
It is so beautiful
So sublime
There's no me in it
There's just life

How backwards
How incredibly backwards
Claim yourself heaven, go ahead
I'm out of the way
I'm ready

The Great Death

I need nothing
I need no one
I am whole

This is simple
This is easy
This is done

If you want this
Come and get it
If you don't
You miss out

I am alone
I am free
I am whole

This is simple
This is silly
This is the end
This is the great death

I am fearless
I am harmless
I am gentle
I am strong

I am nothing
I am everything

I am pure
I am love

Deathless Death

Into an absence of absence I will go
Nothing will be missed
For nothing will be lost
Pure, undistorted and open will be this body
That has carried crosses for far too long

Undaunted by fear I will live
Against rock, stick and stone I will crash
Like a wave that shatters yet remains intact
I will fizzle

If my art is bullshit
Then what is yours
When all you do is play your games
And hide and run from your deepest pains

After death and only after death
Can life begin
So let me die
So I can live

Identityless

The I I can think about isn't real
There is no I
There is nothing
It's always too late
There is no I

Over

The lingering no
Says no to the yes
The permanent yes
Says yes to the no

There is no difference
It doesn't matter
Alone I am
That's simply a fact

Who cares about color?
Who cares about cars?
Who cares about people?
Who cares about stars?

My shallow desires
Just can't be fulfilling
No answers to questions
It's now all in vain

The silly excuses
Can't stop this impulse
To crash and collide
Against a solid illusion
It's done
Over
No going back
It's pointless and silly
To even write

I've Never Been Born

I know I'm a sucker for spiritual nonsense at the
time
I know I'm a sucker for correcting my mistakes
I know I'm totally delusional and insane
But even more important, I know that I've never
been born

I know that I'm hiding in a transcendent haze
I know that I am struggling to come back here
I know I am lost, confused and ridiculous
But even more important, I know that I've never
been born

I know this is yet another stupid poem of mine
I know I can't stop listening to spiritual crap
I know that I'm hiding and running away
But even more important, I know that I've never
been born

I know that I strive for being the best I can be
I know I pursue a bunch of silly things
I know I have preferences that make no difference
at the end
But even more important, I know that I've never
been born

I know that people think a whole bunch of stuff
about me
I know that I think a bunch of stuff about me

I know that thoughts seem to bother me when I believe them
But even more important, I know that I've never been born

I know that I come off like a crazy lunatic
I know that I am disconnected and not here
I know that I am completely asleep at the wheel
But even more important, I know that I've never been born

I know that I don't know anything
I know that I have no idea how I feel
I know that I am terribly somewhere else
But even more important, I know that I've never been born

I know that I don't know if I'll ever come back
I know that I don't know if I'll ever not be crazy
I know that I don't know if I'll always be a buffoon
But even more important, I know that I've never been born

I know that I can't know a thing
I know that I'm not comfortable with knowing that I can't know
I know that I'm ego-driven
But even more important, I know that I've never been born

I know that I am self-indulgent

I know that I make myself sick
I know that I hate delusion and illusion
But even more important, I know that I've never
been born

I know that I am a ball of fear
I know that I am irritating
I know that I don't know what I am talking about
But even more important, I know that I've never
been born

I know that I'll never know
I know that I feel like shit
I know that I'm not trying to figure it out anymore
But even more important, I know that I've never
been born

I know that I don't believe anything
I know that I never want to believe anything
I know that I am tired
But even more important, I know that I've never
been born

I know that I'm terrified of never being Gabriel
again
I know that I'm not Gabriel anymore
I know that I'll never be Gabriel again
But even more important, I know that I've never
been born.

Untitled

I'm in heaven. It has been finally realized.
I am the alpha and the omega.
At last, it has been realized.
There's no going back.

Selfless, Matterless

I've got not self
I've got no eyes
No mouth
No body
No thought
No feeling
Have I been Nirvana'd yet?
I don't know
But I can clearly see
That I'm nothing
That I've got nothing
That I'm empty
Emptier than empty
Less than nothing
Nada
Zip
The mind will see this as terrible
The True I sees it as Itself

Doubtless

Without question
I stand
Like a king that inherited the whole of existence
and beyond
I live

There is no doubt in my system
Zero cynicism
I am that I am
Nothing can shake this
Nothing can touch this

Alone
Alive
In love

Hollow
Empty
Full

Not a single doubt
Not a single question
Not a single thought
Absolutely still

I AM

The Big Awakening

My heart has shattered into a billion pieces
It has exploded into the All
Every fragment is now finally in its rightful place
There is absolutely nothing left of me but openness
I can see again
I am completely humbled
The last thing I expected
Here it is
I am done
My heart is totally here

God Mind Memory

I remember inventing the mountains
Saying let there be life
I remember how it all started
And the joy of it

I remember creating passion
And experiencing experience
I remember being separate
And seeing from a single point

Now I see all
Am all
I remember writing the novel
Creating the story
A great big one
An epic of epics

But now I truly remember
And it's all a fantasy

Alzheimer's

I keep forgetting what I want to write
But it's gotta do with heaven
Oh, I remember
I will not enter dreams anymore
I don't like them
I'm through with dreaming
It's all such a heavy bore
Yuck
I want Truth
Reality
Heaven
Yum

Forms

No thing can bring about bliss
No thing can be owned
No thing lasts
No thing is important
No thing is real

Things want things
Things use things to pretend they own things
Things use things to pretend they "last"
Things use things to pretend they are important
Things use things to pretend they are "real"

Thoughts are things
No thing is real

Life is no thing
Bliss is in nothingness

Sourceless Source

I don't know what writes this
The belief in self has drastically diminished
Self-concern is on its way to non-existence
Worry makes no sense anymore
Questions have no answers
It's all just a joke
It's all just movement in stillness
It's all just a dance in a play
It's not even real
There is nothing
It's all done
Holy cow

Enlightenment

Yesterday I thought there was such a thing as
enlightenment
Yesterday I thought I was a person
Yesterday I thought there was something to do

Today I realize there's no such thing as
enlightenment
Today I realize I have never been a person
Today I realize there's never been anything to do

I am enlightened
I am a person
I have things to do

Yet nothing is true
Nothing is real
It's all a dream

Third Quarter:
Alchemy

Happy Confused Idiot

The spiritual journey
Has obliterated the sense of knowing
I have no investment in my head anymore
All that's up there is hogwash

I don't know who to listen to
Where to go
Or what to do
I'm dumbfounded

I don't know who I am
What I want
Or what I need

I'm faking being happy
Confused
And most of all
An idiot

Soft Clear Confession

I can tell you my loudest celebration
My brassiest of screams of joy
I can make such bold noise

But a soft clear confession scares me
And tenses me up
I feel a little shy about it

I can be a loud mouth
But a soft mouth I'm not too sure
The layers of protection come up

And the most I do is choke

This has been my story
One that I've been fascinated with
But enough is enough
And now I can whisper to you
My soft and clear confession

The Fool's Runaway

I sold her for cash and recognition
My heart's ears closed
What a fool I've been
Thinking fame meant greatness

I didn't respect her fears
I projected all my baggage onto her
My queen, my true beauty
What a beast I've been

Wrapped in a dress
In a still image I saw her
As I listened to our song
Salt and blood rushed to my eyes
And bitter collapse ensued

My pumpkin
My dusty
My dance
Alone I sit
Without her
With my cash and recognition

Careful what you wish for
Is all I gotta say

Damaged Dream Debris

A dream that drove my existence shattered
Of course, over another dream
Then a no-dream came in and it damaged it all

There is something that is not dreaming
Because it doesn't need to
The thing that dreams must dream

The dreamer awakens
And all that's left is lucidity
Awakeness
Bare reality

All But Me

The walls are wiser than me
My sneakers too
So is my floor
And no doubt my dog as well

The trees are way more awake and aware
The wind knows the secret
I pretend like I know something
And the truth is just that I know nothing

My deodorant knows all about peace
My socks know all about freedom
The water I drink is enlightened
I'm the only one behind

I don't listen to people anymore
They don't know what they're talking about
But the air I breathe laughs and gets it
So I rather breathe in and out
Instead of listening to a person

Tribute To My Teacher

The saint that showed me love
Mustered all his patience
Gave me a gentle, truthful look
That transformed my eternity

He who didn't play the above or below game
Because he simply knows who he is
He who actually and truthfully is who he is
Just looks me in the eye and smiles
And shows me a reflection of myself

He who tries not
But simply is
He is the true saint and savior
My heart's true love and desire

He who wants nothing of me
He who wants nothing of himself
He who just is
Is the greatest teacher of all
And he need not do a damn thing
But just be

Powerless

I don't have my powers anymore
I can't feel good or bad about myself anymore
There is no myself anymore
I have no opinions
I know nothing
I trust nothing
Believe nothing
Think nothing
I am healed
Sane
Free
With no powers
Finally

Baby Wail

I just want to be heard
Understood
Loved
Agreed with
Comforted
Why isn't anyone giving it to me?
Where is it?

My Grace

They wouldn't let me speak my truth
They wouldn't let me say a word that went against
them
All I heard was shut up
They wouldn't let me make a move
The wouldn't let me see a light
They kept me shut, sealed and scared
But I forged on through
And so did they
And it became a battle
Where stuff was flying all over the place
And I was scared but poised
I couldn't own myself
I couldn't perceive what I perceived
I was always told to shut up
The pain still lives with me
But it's okay
It only happens when I believe my thoughts about
it
But my body still cries
I still bleed
And it's okay
Because it's all grace

Power

The power that I've yearned for
Has always been within
Trapped in an illusion, confused inside a dream

I am all I've ever wanted
I am exactly that
I am beauty, grace and power

I am love and compassion
I am song and I am dance
I am nothing and everything

I am blown away by myself
I can't believe I'm this much
I am infinite, eternal

I am presence
I am divine
I am incredible, I am amazing, I am shocking

The beauty of myself can't be outdone
I am in love with myself
With every cell, every neuron, every thought

I am goodness
I am true, I am real
I am you and I am me

I am nothing

I am everything
I am always and forever

Facing Inner Demons

I'm facing my demons
It almost seems counterintuitive
It feels uncomfortable
No wonder why no one goes into this voluntarily
It fucking sucks
Well, that's relative, but that's the feeling
Who wants to uncover the demons within
Like finding out how destructive you are?
And how arrogant?
How you literally think you know everything?
It's not for sissies
It's real stuff
It's gritty
It is literally facing the actual, true and real demons
Not so fun in the beginning
But it is starting to get kind of fun and exciting to
me
Although scary as shit
I'm ready!

Daily I Die

Daily I die
Chunk by chunk
Bit by bit
It's all going into Oneness

The illusions of separation
Are seen through more and more
What sense is there in doing?
What sense is there in anything?
Not yet
Not yet

I am the One
You are the One
What clouds it?
The clouds need not leave
But a seeing through does occur
Which obliterates the sense of clouds
It's all there
But it's all empty

It's all One
This is beyond the idea
This is the felt sense
This is a realization that goes beyond thought and
feeling
It is true knowing
It is God

True Love

True love shatters all ideas
It melts questions
It obliterates doubt
It gets you up in the middle of the night and it
moves you to create
It frees you completely
It liberates thoughts
It opens the gates
It is simple, clear and silent
It is passionately active and creative
It is the energy that drives existence
It is all you see, all you are

Allow

Allow yourself to be loved
Allow yourself to be touched
Allow yourself to be heard
Allow yourself to be where you are at

The power for this to liberate is immense
Do you want to be liberated?
Or would you rather keep your shell?

You are the Guru
When you allow yourself to be found
When you allow yourself to be free
The credit is yours
Let yourself go

The Void

There's no one there
There's nothing there
Where I go to scream
Where I go to cry
Where I go to beg
There's nothing there
There's no one there
All there seems to be there is just me
There is no one there
There is nothing there
So I yell, scream and cry and lose my voice
And get no answer
And I burn and burn
And no response
There is nothing there
It's empty, silent, nonexistent
No one to look, no one to care
No one to put on a show for
Nothing

It's just me and my show

Teen to Twenties

When I play with Spotty I wanna be a dog
When I chill with Kermit I want to be a frog
When I dance with Mom I want to have five kids
When I talk to Dad I want to be a king

When I learn from Adya I want to shave my head
When I look at Mooji I want to gain some weight
When I hear some Gangaji I want to be a girl
When I enjoy some Elton I want to be so gay

When I vocalize with Mark I want to grow my hair
When I visit Susie I want to shave it off
When I go to the movies I want to be Brad Pitt
When I sleep too much I feel like a lazy piece of
shit

When I work real hard I fear ending up like Mom
and Dad
When I look outside I want to be a tree
When I sing a song I want to sound like Ricky
When I read some Einstein I want to be like him

When I think of Jesus I want to carry a cross
When I hear about Buddha I want to give it all up

Jealous Of My Heroes

Like a small child
The only way to point my gaze is up
To look above me

I get jealous
I admire
I get embarrassed

I want that

I look up to my heroes
And that is every person
That is not me

I so want that
I don't want this

I Am It

I don't want the future
I don't want the past
I don't want the present
I don't want

I am life
I am God
I am this

I soak in this moment
And it is exquisite
I can't possibly suffer
This is exactly what I want
This is what I am
This is exactly what I am

I am in love
Completely
With everything

This is it
This is so it
It is grace
It is God
And I am it

Embrace

Hold yourself close
Kiss
Embrace the human
Give it a break

Listen and go
Dance, make a show
Be what you are
Stop living the lie

Breathe it all in
Take it all out
Cry if you want
Laugh if you like

Life is a gift
Everything is
Sing your own song
Dance your own dance

Last of Prayers

I'm terrified of myself
Terrified of being human
Terrified of being an actor
I'm none of these things
Yet there's no reason to fear them
What the heck is the problem?
Where does all this fear come from?
It's immense, enormous, overbearing
I don't want to step into the roles
I'm afraid of getting stuck and attached to them
I don't want it to happen
God give me strength to be weak
I'm tired of hiding, of pretending
I can't be brave
I don't know how to do it
God give me strength
God give me what it takes to be
I'm through with myself
I'm done as can be
I give up heaven, I give up hell
I give it all up
Although my guru told me it's not about that
What do I do?
Where do I go?
What am I?

The Change of Season

We mortals are part of all that's transient
All form moves to the beat of the same drum
There isn't a single manifestation that isn't affected
by the swings of totality
There is no such thing as structural stability

A flower withers when the season doesn't favor it
A dog sheds its coat when it becomes obsolete
The wardrobe suffers changes
And hibernation and migration take place

It's wonderful to be conscious
And see the cosmic shifts
Experience all the cycles
And see the falling leaves

Transformation isn't always pleasant
Neither is life
But a being that's in alignment
Can experience depth and truth

As the shells start to collapse
In response to a season's change
Reality starts to break in
And triumph once again

The fearlessness of falling
Starts to dawn within the brave
As those who are frightened harden

And hold on to their shell

My shell is way too broken
My heart is way too open
My trust is too enormous
I see the light again

Slice me
Dice me
Cut through me
For I am fearless and transparent

Life is a Matter of Heart

The creative, loving channels
Mind and Heart
Were once a balanced team

Shock happened
The Heart got spooked
And the door got shut

The heart wants to love
Wants to live
The mind wants to create
Wants to serve

Remember that day
When you concluded you couldn't 't take it
anymore?
Look around you
It's a new day, a new time, a new dawn

Check if your heart can take it now
Open and test the waters
And if you get spooked again
Keep testing these new waters

Seek to be born again
Reclaim true fulfillment of open mind and open
heart
You might just be able
To fulfill your mission of love this time around

Wake up, silly

Dance 'Til The End

On my last lines
On my last deeds
Dancing with death
That consumes me

Destroying myself
At full throttle
Nothing will be left
Except what is

Dancing the dance until the end
Burning all of me
Irrational
But it wants me

So I will surrender
For love

The Way Out

If I try hard enough
I just might
Convince myself
That nothing's wrong
That nothing's ever happened

I might realize that
All is well
And that all my stories
Are a broken spell

I might just be free
If that's what I want
But I'll stay hypnotized
If that's my desire

Will I keep selling my soul to the stories?
That have perhaps never been real
The only way to find out
Is letting go of the training wheels

Do I want to learn to ride without them?
Do I want to remain feeling safe?
Safe and numb
To the dance on the big stage

What do I want?
Where am I going?
Who am I?

Is it all just a story

Step outside the mud
And get familiar with the unfamiliar
The mud will always be there
In case you ever want it back
Except you might discover
It was all just a façade

What do you want?
Where are you going?
Who are you?
Is it all just a story?

Do you have a choice?
Do you want to find out?
Or would you rather keep hiding
In your fear and your doubt?

Is this just pretty?
Or is it filled with truth?
Is it all just nicety?
Or is something in this pure?

What are the implications
Of living this poem?
Are there any
Or is it all just a story?

Daddy

Day one you were God
Day two you were a fool
Day three you were an asshole
Today you are a man

Day one I was a child
Day two I was a teenager
Day three I was an immature adult
Today I am a man

I see you as you are
I see me as I am
And I can't stop crying
And it doesn't bother me anymore

Full Moon:
Integration

Warm

It'd be nice
If you came
And hung out for a while
Out here
Where there is nothing

You can go back whenever you want
But it'd be nice
If you lost the fear of hanging loose
In the middle of nowhere

It's a place inside
Where there are no rules
No shoulds or shouldn'ts
No ifs or buts

Just nothing
Not the nothing you imagine
The nothing you can't imagine
It'd be nice to meet you here
Where there is no difference between you and I
It'd be nice

Open Chakras

My root chakra has spoken
It's told me who you are
It tells me about your chaos
It informs me about your wars

The truth that is always simple
Has the power to set you free
It's the willingness to be simple
That sets off your wings

It has always been so gentle
So embarrassingly simple
Yet complexity has seduced you
For far too many lifetimes

Are you chakras open enough
This time around
To allow humility to crush you fully
Or is the fear and rage greater

Ignorance is not bliss
Ignorance is hell
Open your chakras and let yourself be fully
crushed
For that little self that struggles to be in charge

Is but a figment of your imagination

Real Woman

The Goddess of Love
Gave birth to five schizophrenics
That change their minds every other minute
She did this for nothing less than Pure Love

She gave them paths to self-realization
She gave them an opportunity to experience
The pains and pleasures of life

And she let them go just in time
The Master Goddess of Autonomy
The Divine Goddess goes in and out of insanity
And realizes herself every few minutes

A Good Woman
A Sincere Woman
A Real Woman
My Mother

True Power

If you are reading this
You have true power
Power to realize
That you are what you want
Now

All else is bullshit
You know this
Stop making excuses
Stop talking shit

If you are reading this
You are really lucky
You know this
Stop pretending you don't know what I'm talking
about

If you are reading this
You are afraid
You know this
Stop pretending like you are not

The true power you are is infinite
You know this
It's unbounded
It gets you exactly what you want

You are tired of playing victim
You know this

If you need my help
I am here and I can really help you
You know this

Stability Prayer

No one will ever convince me that life isn't
sublimely beautiful
No one will ever convince me that everything isn't
a gift
No one will ever shake my conviction that life is
the maximum expression of grace
No one will ever make me doubt my power
No one will ever blur my clarity
No one will ever obscure my beauty

No one will ever touch me with their negative
bullshit
No one will ever come close to me with their
nonsense

Fragmented souls will not take me on their trips

I am all I ever want
And this life is nothing but mind blowing
This life is all I have ever dreamed and beyond
No one will touch this
For it is who I am

Chmurka

How can a soul so tender
At times be so rough
Yet still be so lovable
And sublimely soft

Who is this Polish angel
That has come into my life
They say his name is Dariusz
But I think he's just pure light

He says there are no voices
While I know there are
But never ever stronger
Than his beautiful heart

Who is this lovely guardian
This masterful soul
That has given me the platform
To spread my wings and grow

Kocham cie chmurka
My soul is your soul
I thank you every second
For your magical touch

Eminence

The body is in me
I am in the body
I am the One
The body moves in me
I move in the body
I am

I am all there is, was and will be
I am everyone
I am everything

I am it

Trance

The swing of your pendulum
No longer induces me into a trance
The smell of your rotten flowers
No longer appeals to me

I'm no fool
I'm done with the game
There's no more playing
Because I'm no longer here

And neither are you

The Mind That I'm Not

It calls me over and over
And it grabs my attention almost every time
A perfect seductress
That drags me into its pit

I look outside and nothing has value
I buy into it and it's all virtually true
I am fooled, duped and bamboozled
Over and over

But the daisy outside is real
And yet the mind that I'm not
Sells me a story
And I buy it almost every time

I'm in love with detraction
Because it frees me from what I'm not
I'm in love with the mind
Because it's the coolest game in town

But games are games
And games will be games
And the game is over
And I quit

Sweet, Sweet Soldier

War's anything that's cruel
And preps the soil
For the birth of a long revolution
That we can't foresee

And we all know
That at the onset and in the midst
It sure ain't pretty

I feel what you went through
And boy was your war tough
Finding your superior on the ground
Obviously killed you too

Yet you marched on
You sweet, sweet soldier
And fed so many
As you kept bumbling on

Your mitzvahs are plenty
Your heart is infinite
So tender and encased
And so, so perfect

Thanks for letting me have the fruit
My Amazing Father

Who Would I Be Without Myself?

Without the sage-like silence of my own soul
Who would I be?
Without the impartial voice of pure consciousness
What would be of me?

A conformist, I never could be
My inner voice speaks too loudly
Unique and authentic
Only the voice of my heart
The light that I am grows

Each time I hear it
I seek nothing
For I lack nothing
This, my voice knows

Without my voice I'd have to depend on foreign voices
I would have to use songs and feelings that I did not write or feel
I would have to depend on advice of beings that most likely failed

No one knows more than I what I'm here for
No one knows more than I what I want
No one knows more than I who I am
Not my mother, not my father - they don't touch my own essence

No one knows exactly what I need to hear as I do
No one is more enlightened for my own life than I
am

The same applies to you
If you have the courage to realize

Children need authority
Adults don't

Free yourself and write your own songs
Stop borrowing feelings from others
Create your own life
Do not use others to create it for you

Create your own religion
Just like the great ones did
Create your own genre
Your own book

Stop borrowing already
Live your life from your heart

After all...
Who would you be without yourself?
... Absolutely nobody

Happiness

If you are wondering
Or are about to wonder
Why I write this
I'll be honest
I have no clue

I am happy
You have no idea
I have no idea
It's beyond idea

I can only guess
That this is also possible
For you and all of humankind

Do you want it?
Beyond just saying you want it?
Or do you want something else?
What is it you want?

Find out
Because if what you want is this
You can have it
I dare you to feel the truth in this simple poem

Big Fat Joke

Somewhere inside
My being is dancing
Laughing at the joke
That it finally caught onto

Where have I been all this time
Thinking stuff up
Clouding the view
Of absolute purity

This is just a big fat joke
That few people get
It makes the joke funnier
It's all just a big fat zero

Even less than that
Yeah, cause-and-effect is true
But it's happening inside of the joke
The joke that can't be named

And it's all created
By the waves
Of a big fat laugh

My Most Powerful Bait

Let's be cowards
And escape
Let's leave it all behind

Let's fulfill
Life's true mission
Which we know nothing of

The fear is endless
But who gives a shit
Let's just fucking leave it all

It's all garbage anyway
It's old news
It's predictable and repetitive

Let's do this
Because this time around
We can

And we just might get away with it
Let's go
Are you not game?

Sex Love

I want to take her to the clouds
Make her feel so proud
Kiss her toes without a doubt
Watch her cry when I'm about

See her smile
When I'm inside
Hear her moan against a sigh

Touch her soul
Kiss her cheek
Spin her around
And sing a bit

I want to love her
Fully
In and out
Push a bit gently
Get it all in

Leave her beside me
As I
Need her

Clarity

Nothing can push me
Nothing can pull me
Nothing can move me
I am still

Everything pushes me
Everything pulls me
Everything moves me
I am movement

The flow is forever here
Nothing sticks
There is no resistance
I am free

I am the raging river emerging out of the still pond
Dying in the still pond
I am clear

I'm not good
I'm not bad
I simply am

Embodied

Needless
Desireless
Entirely fulfilled
By myself
All alone
Who wants this?
This is scary
This is true
This is it

But then what?
Oh, nothing
Just everything
For the very first time
Again

I'm enough
Holy shit
This is stupid
This is sick
All the looking
For more outside
This is insane
I am all
I am it
Relaxation
Beyond definition
Nirvana
Moksha

Freedom
Liberation
Enlightenment
Everything

Are you kidding me?
This is it?
Wow this is obvious!

Dawning: Nirvana

Step 2

The outfit is way too small for what you are
What you are is infinite, unbounded, eternal
When there is confusion
The outfit longs to be divine
But it can't
Because it already is

Realizing you are not the outfit
Fully liberates you
And frees you
From the longing to become

And becoming happens naturally
As it always has

The Force

The yearning for freedom is not rational
It doesn't take no for an answer
It is insidious, it does not stop
It keeps pulling and pulling and it has no
consideration
For anyone or anything but freedom itself

There is no way out of the pull
No way in
It's just a pull
That leads the dance

Nothing can be done
Nothing can be undone
It just happens
And it can take any form

But it happens
No matter what

And you're left
Free
Without the need to understand
Without the need to reconcile
Without needs

It makes no sense to the mind
But it is the only thing that's true

Limitation is only an appearance
That gets you to the realization of true freedom
No matter what

The Light Within

The Light Within knows
It is fearless
It is open, loving, caring and engaged
It is present
It is powerful
It is perfect
Divine
It informs life
It informs the heart
It informs the mind
It is the Light Of God
And that is what you are

The Deepest Calling

The deepest yearning
Of forgotten nature
Is to realize itself
And find the choiceless realm
What we all long for is for having no choice
No choice but to be
Choice is a burden of burdens
No choice
Just this
That's the light of your being
That's who and what you are
Realize
Now

That

It's more simple than healing
More simple than love
More simple than inspiration

It's more obvious than awareness
More humble than humility
More welcoming than the coziest welcome
More present than presence

It's simpler than a tear
Simpler than a smile
More real than reality
More clear than clarity

More constant than constancy
More reliable than reliability
More sublime than heaven
It's not graspable, it's not personal, it's not even
beautiful
It's more enlightened than light itself

Way, way less than nothing
And here it is, for few to see

It's way more silent than silence itself
Are you quiet enough to see it?

It's brighter than light itself
A lot more empty than emptiness

It's not heaven, it's not hell
It's not in between
It's not shocking, it's not emotional, it's not impacting
It does melt the wickedest witches though
It's not water, water is too much
Have you found it yet?

The Other Side

There is nothing on the other side
Nothing good, nothing bad
Nothing indifferent
Nothing that's nothing

It's an empty play
Devoid of meaning
Devoid of movies, devoid of films

It's an empty that's so empty
That it's not even empty
And there's nothing to it
But this

Gone And Here

Gone is the past me that's false
Gone is the myopic teenager from the center
Gone is the uninformed child from the control base

Here is Spirit
Nirvana

Gone is the hot too hot
The cold too cold
Gone is the extremist from the center
Here is the human

www.ingramcontent.com/pod-product-compliance
Lightning Source LLC
Chambersburg PA
CBHW032037040426
42449CB00007B/922